GLYN GOODE

# NO BEACH LEFT TO *Walk on*

*Poems of Reflection*

# NO BEACH LEFT TO *Walk on*

## Poems of Reflection

**MEMOIRS**
Cirencester

Published by Memoirs

MEMOIRS
PUBLISHING

25 Market Place, Cirencester, Gloucestershire, GL7 2NX
info@memoirsbooks.co.uk  www.memoirspublishing.com

ISBN: 978-1-909304-50-5

Printed in England

To my daughters Stephanie and Nicole and my son Christian.

Without them I am nothing.

# Table of Contents

FROM A LITTLE RAIN

FOREVER GONE

DIFFERENT

A LONG NIGHT

HELLO

TOO LONG HERE

WHY GOD, WHY?

HABIT

LOVE LOST

I AM

OPEN YOUR MIND

A HARD CHOICE

A HAPPY MAN

SAY NO TO GREEN

LEAPFROG

SHORT CUT

THE MESSENGER

NO MORE SUMMER WINE

THE SMILE

A BEAUTIFUL FEELING

NO REGRETS

THE MAN WHO NEVER WAS

CITY WHIZZKIDS

NO ETIQUETTE

NO REGRETS

# FOREVER

Soon it will be dawn
I see her shadow crossing the lawn
Friends say she's not there
But what's that rustle in the air
The leaves in the trees flicker
While below daffodils bicker
Clouds are crossing the face of the moon
She will be here soon

I rush to the door
To see my love once more
She has not left me
She never will
The wind had fallen, it's now still
As I walk from the door
I can hear her call
Come join me my love
I am here in the clouds above.

# SLIPPERY TOAD AHEAD

Strolling along a country road
I found my way hindered
By an enormous toad!
Thinking he was hurt
And I being a caring soul
I stopped and offered him help.
'Are you alright?' I ask
'Oh yes, thank you,' he croaks.
'By the way, before you pass
Have you paid your road tax?'
'But dear sir, I do say
I have no car
So I have not rode
So I have no tax to pay
But here's a kiss and a cuddle
And I will be on my way.'

After a while I met Mrs Hare
'Goodday Mrs Hare, I do say
Isn't this a lovely day?'
'Yes, it is,' she says
'Did you meet Mr Toad on your way?'
'Yes, I did,' I reply.
'Did you pay his tax?'
'Oh no, I gave him a kiss
And went on my way.'
'That was for the best!
Don't bother about him,
He's just trying to feather his own nest.'

'Come, Mrs Hare, let's have a cup of tea.'
'Now that would be nice!
There's a café just around the bend:
It's owned by my friend.
Her name is Mrs Mole
And it's called "Toad in the Hole"!'
After we had our tea
I thanked Mrs Mole and Mrs Hare.
Mrs Hare said, 'Have you further to roam?'
'No, I am nearly there,' said I
As I wished them both goodbye
And went on my way home.

As I approached home
I saw this figure standing alone.
'Oh no, not you again, Mr Toad!'
'Yes, sorry,' he says
'But again I have to ask,
Can you please give to my tax?
For I am trying to raise enough money
So I can build a tunnel
So all of us toads
Can safely cross the road.'

# MY LOVE

Blue skies your smiling face
Make my heart race
The sparkle in your eyes
Your soft gentle sighs
My hand you gently squeeze
Bless you when I sneeze
When things are tough
You just shrug
Your love is enough
No need my love for fears
I will kiss away your tears

Lying in bed side by side
Heart bursting with pride
Such a look of beauty on your face
I'm so lucky to be here in this place
You're so gentle, so mild
It's Christmas again and I'm a child
Presents to open and view
God, how I love you!

# ROOM WITH A VIEW

As I look from my window
What do I see?
Tenement houses in front of me
Chimney pots, pigeons and crow
With all the pictures they can throw
A train trundling by
Vapour trails in the sky
Burnt out car, discarded chair
Smoke drifting in the air
Dogs howling, give me love
Bottles thrown from above
Women out on the street
Bills trying to meet
Kids kicking a can
Out of here they plan
Inner city, inner stink
No room here to think
No warm soft glow
Looking from my window.

# CHANGING TIMES

This fastly changing electronic world
Leaves my mind in a whirl
I've no computer, no mobile phone
No email, I don't work from home
I've no time for this www dot com
It's so impersonal
It's not where I'm coming from
To meet people face to face
To hold and embrace
This is being part of the human race

The sight of a heron at early morn
The smell of a newly mown lawn
The joy of seeing a new born child
Horses running free and wild
Walking with your dog on a beach
A loving kiss on the cheek
These are all pleasures
No computer can teach.

# HERE FOR YOU

I hurt to see the pain in your eyes
Or to hear the despair in your sighs
No smile to lift the pain
Tears falling like rain
The anguish in your face
It's not you it's out of place
But at the end of the tunnel
There will be light
For I am here for you
Together we will end your awful plight.

# STRANGE DAYS

You have strange days
Funny little ways
Days of pain
Nights of joy
One day brash
The next coy
One day you smile
The next you frown
One day you're up
Then you're down
You have strange days
Funny little ways.

# MY LOVE FOR MY DAUGHTERS

Do swallows fly
With swifts on high
In the day, is not the sky light
And dark in the night?
When we are apart
Does it not break my heart
As the tides ebb and flow.
Does my soul not glow?
Is my mind not in a whirl
With love and joy for my girls?


# OVER THE SEA

From here I have to move away
New places I need to find
Laze under blue skies and warm sun
Before my life is done
To meet different races
See their smiling faces
Gentle seas rolling onto a white beach
All this is within my reach!

Different cultures, different styles
Browse in the markets for a while
Dusky maidens in native skirts
Me in my Hawaiian shirt
All this is available to me
If I just sail away over the sea!

# THE LONELY BEAR

He walks where no one dare
The perilous path to his lair
One poor soul tried in vain
Never to be seen again…
His long hair wet and matted
His empty stomach knotted
The fish are long gone
The berries all done
There's a cold chill in the air
That follows the path of the lonely bear.


# YOU BROUGHT ME LIGHT

In my life was darkness
You brought me light
As with a blind man
Given his sight
You gave my life a reason
Like spring is a season
Afresh and new
My love for you
Knows no bounds
For you turned my life around.

# ONLY CLOUDS

Thoughts of you
Are words unspoken
A thought just a token
Arrows to your heart broken
Today my mind has awoken
Now I can see your love
Were but clouds above.


# THOUGHTS

Walking alone along the beach
With the tide rushing in
Trying to reach
Swirling mists caress the sea
Voices calling out to me
Tendrils reaching into my inner mind
Answers trying to find
Awaken thoughts from the deep
Secrets no longer to keep
Visions from the past drift by
Thoughts as clouds in the sky.

# ME

The me you see
That is not me
For the me I am
Is another man
I am not what you see
For I cannot be
The person you see
For I can only be me.


# DANCE AND ROMANCE

The beauty of dancing
Is in the romancing
You hold your partner around her waist
Her sweet lips you long to taste
You look longingly into her eyes
And twinkling stars appear
The band is playing
But you do not hear

You glide across the dance floor
As if you were floating on air
The dance floor is full
But for you no one else is there
Light gently falls from above
But you don't seem to see
For you are hopelessly in love.

# MY FIRST LOVE

Oh so many years ago when I was a young
boy of sixteen or so I met a young girl of
beauty beyond my dreams. She was so gentle
and lithe, three years less than me.
It was love at first sight for her and for me
We were in each other's thoughts day and night.
We pined for each other when we were out of sight
She of sweet nature and face and me, I
thought I was out of place. But I know she
loved me with all her heart, so why did I cause
us to part?
Oh, stupid boy in his teens, why oh why did
you ruin her dreams?
We live our lives as best we deem and there's
no point in chasing yesterday's dream. But why,
oh why, sweet love of my heart, did I cause us to part?
These thoughts have plagued my mind and
after all these years no answers do I find.

# FIRST LIGHT

Floating in a swirling sea
Enclosed by walls all around me
Heaving, pushing, trying to break free
Please cut this cord that binds me!
Free at last after such a long time
Now I need to clear my mind
For this new world I've yet to find
Out of darkness into light
Open my eyes for my first sight.

# LITTLE JENNY WREN

Little Jenny, little Wren
You're such a dainty thing
All fluster and wing
Darting here, darting there
Thro' branches of trees
Peeking thro' the leaves
Forward and back, up and down
You're such an acrobatic clown!

# STOLEN LOVE

Alone I walk on an autumn day
Loneliness leads the way
Heart stolen, broken in two
Oh, how I miss you!
Tears, I cannot stem the flow
Why, oh why did you go?
My head full of fears
Why won't it rain?
Wash away these tears
In bed alone at night
Future full of fright
Soul filled with doubt
My fears to shout
No longer make me fret
I've loved you since first we met.


# THROWN AWAY

There are times
I have found
That my heart
You have bound
Tied in a knot
Then thrown away
And then forgot.

# SO FAR AWAY

You're so far away from me
Far away over the sea
Oh my love, I miss you so
The blush in your cheeks
Every time we meet
Your sweet shy smile
That sparkles in your face
Oh, to hold you once again
And feel your warm embrace!
When you're away I feel so alone
Oh my love, please hurry home!

# ALONE

I speak
No one hears
My words
Just disappear
I cry
Who wipes my tears?
I hurt
Who will care?
My thoughts
Who will share?
I pass away
Who will be there?
Alone in my grave
Who will offer a prayer?

# BEN

His spirit floating from on high
Into my soul it seeps
With a thankful sigh
His memory locked forever
Deep in my heart to keep
My Ben for you
I still weep.

# STORMY SEAS

Raging demons in the sky
Rolling seas in a race
By the ship rushing by
Driving rain slashing the face
Lightning flashes drums of thunder
Quivering masts all asunder
Rushing water swamping decks
Nothing to keep feet in check
Weary seamen lowering sail
All efforts to no avail
Oh, evil tempest on high
Please hurry, hurry by!

# A WALK BY A COUNTRY STREAM

Willows gently weep upon a slow moving stream
As it winds its way thro' pastures green
Just a sigh away nestle trees
A soft breeze caresses their leaves
In midstream patiently he stands
Noble and grey the heron fishes
But no rod touches his hands
Swallows swooping on high
Perform an avian ballet in the sky

Shrubs blanketed by a spider's web
Spun finer than filigree
Trap a fly, a curious bee
As the sun sets in a golden sky
It's with a long sigh
I reluctantly stop my roam
And slowly wend my way home.

# SUNDAY ON
# THE VILLAGE GREEN

Old men in deckchairs sleeping
The crack of leather against willow they are missing
Batsmen runs they are seeking
With umpires on watch order keeping
Young girls with ropes skipping
Young lads with bats just wishing

Swallows dancing in the sky
Ducks just waddling by
Could things be more serene
Than a sunny Sunday afternoon on the village green
With cucumber sandwiches and glasses of beer
But more's the pity it's all in yesteryear.

# VISION

I've had a vision, a dream
A nightmare of the future
Oh boy, it's not as it would seem
Rivers will still flow
But they carry a deadly glow
There will be no skies of blue
No fluffy clouds of white
Giving the world light
Rivers of mercury, zinc and lead
All life therein long dead.

Foaming seas of detergent waste
No tender morsels for man to taste
No more fields of swaying corn
Mixed with thistle and thorn
No more acres of endless wood
Just black plains where forests once stood
A few humans scattered here and there
Though for not much longer
For there's no food left to share.

# WORDS

Words crafted by the ages
As thoughts on pages
By a blacksmith smelt
Caress the tongue almost felt
Words sharper than tempered steel
Sharp enough to make one reel
Words come and pass you by
A shrug, a sigh
Gone in the blink of an eye.


# FISH

Strolling along the seashore
Suddenly a thought comes to the fore
Green, yellow, red, blue
Fish have so varied a hue
But in the near future
Will they be mine to view?
Will their existence be secure?
No!  Because of the greed of man
Who cannot see what's before his eyes
Fish cannot survive

But will it end there?
Oh no! Then there's the bear.

# SPIDER

Oh spider, there in your web
Such a fragile trap you do spread
You have no deadlines to meet
Just hope to trap something to eat!


# THE WRITER

I am a writer
I have a story to tell
Your mind I will control
Force you to read every line
Take you on a trip to heaven
When you think things are well
I'll take you on a fast trip to hell
When you think there's no more in store
I'll make you read
Just one page more.

# THE RACE

Mile upon mile on tired legs
Please give me rest, your body begs
So for a few hours you relieve the load
But come the morning it's back on the road
Push those pedals down, ever down
Force those wheels round and round
Can't give up now, must win the race
Rivers of sweat flood down your face
Down mountain roads you speed
Your safety you give no heed
You give all, take every chance
All this to win
The Tour de France!

# A FORLORN DREAM

To walk thro' fields of green
By hedgerows where wildlife teems
To stroll along river banks
And meandering country streams
To breathe fresh clean air
This is what I dream
To stroll along without a care
But I have this fear
This cannot now be mine
Because of the demands
Of this modern time.

# UNSPOKEN LOVE

I weep but you do not see
The pain that surrounds me
My heart you have broken
By words you have not spoken
I hurt, can you not see?
Your blindness is killing me.


# GOLDEN AGE OF STEAM

Trains driven by steam
An enthusiast's dream
On the platform they are waiting
Notebooks they are opening
Mouths opening with a joyous cry
As the monster roars by
Black smoke belching from the engine stack
Black grass growing alongside the track
Washing hanging on the line
Now covered in grit, soot and grime
Enough to make the housewife scream
The Golden Age of steam!

# 1984 (ODE TO THE WORKING MAN)

Speak when you are spoken to
It doesn't matter what you think
It doesn't matter what you say
We will decide what's right for you
Each and every day.

# WITHDRAWAL SYMPTOMS OF A VEGETARIAN

There it lies on the plate
A nice thick juicy steak
With mushrooms, tomatoes, chips and peas
Oh yes, please, please, please!

Its black skin shining
Its insides full of blood
Is anything more enticing
Than a plate of cheese and black pud?

Turkey full of sage and onion stuffing
Roast beef and Yorkshire pudding
Leg of lamb and mint sauce
Or pork as the main course
But whatever I eat
I will not go back to meat.

# QUEST

Gentle flakes of snow
Chill my soul as I wander
Where I do not know
Like a tramp in the night
Thro' cities and towns
In an endless flight
I search for wrongs to put right
Like a knight in armour shining bright
Thro' driving snow or rain
I go to ease the pain
But whose pain do I try to ease?
Or is it my conscience I try to appease?

# LOVE APPLE

I'm a tomato man
Off the vine out of a can
With pickles and cheese
A slice of ham
I like them toasted
I like them grilled
One way I haven't tried
Tomatoes fried.

# ONLY ME

I am often called a fool, a clown
People try to pull me down
My poems they don't understand
Perhaps it's their own doubts they sow
For they don't seem to know
I can only write when I feel
Things that I see
For the poems that I write
Are only a reflection of me.


# GROWING OLD

To see children playing
Hear them laughing
It makes one sad
To be ageing…

# SUMMER MORN

Rising sun in a pale blue sky
Swifts flying on high
Poppies from the roadside grow
Sparrows nesting in a hedgerow
Fields of swaying yellow corn
Sheer delights of an early morn
Climbing mice on slender stalks
Insects with their incessant talk
Foxes searching for an early meal
While up above martins reel
Speckles of dew on summer flowers
Their petals opening to the sun
A summer's day has just begun.

# JUST ONCE MORE

Waves gently caressing the seashore
So peaceful the sound
As it retreats with a shush
To return once more
In its eternal rush
Wind blowing gently thro' the trees
Caressing the leaves
As with an artist's brush
Glades of primroses and bluebells by the shore
Just to see and hear these things once more
Before the final closing of this life's door.

# DEATH THROES

Oh Earth of beauty, Earth of grace
You are being raped by the human race
Forests of evergreens, such a delight
Bringing to my life joy and light
Majestic mountains, huge roiling seas
Polluted by an animal who overbreeds
Slaughtering all in its path
Nothing escapes its wrath.

Nuclear power stations built in haste
No thought given to its waste
Oh, I despair, I'm losing hope
The planet is choking in smoke.

The human animal is in a desperate race
To find a new home in outer space
Because the human animal doesn't seem to know
You only reap what you sow.

# JUKE BOX

Go to the pub for a quiet drink
Ha ha! That's what you think!
Buy a beer and take a seat
And hope this isn't where the young meet
Oh no! Here they are thirsty and hot!
Buy a drink, put a coin in the slot
And on comes the Juke Box!
Thumping beat blasts the ears
All my worst fears!
It's not loud, so I am told
It must be me getting old!

# MY HOSPITAL BED

Again, once more I'm here
Lying in pain and fear
Here in my hospital bed
My mind full of dread
My arm attached to a saline drip
Like a clock tick tick tick
Body racked by pain
Could things be any worse?
Oh no, here comes the nurse
With that needle again!

# LAMPPOST

Tall and slim it stands
Casting its light all around
Like a sentinel with one arm on high
Brightening the night sky
In the mist it stands like a ghost
The humble lamppost.


# THE GARDEN FENCE

Very much maligned by some
This traditional old English custom
A bowl of sugar or a tea bag
Or just a good old chinwag
A place to lean and air your views
Catch up on the local news
It plays a major role in society
For some the garden fence is a necessity.

# WHY

They are gone now, passed away
Relatives, friends mourn them, but not me
For they are to be envied
For now they are free
No more doubts, no more worries
As they say, home free!
But the relatives, friends, you and me
We're still here
With all the worries, all the fears
You are born, you live, you die,
It makes one wonder why.


# A GROWING LAD

Such a sweet innocent face
Broken biscuits all over the place
No chance to lie in bed
The young lad needs to be fed
Tired? Oh, what a shame!
Come on, I want a game
Ladies' knickers he does steal
Around the washing basket he does reel
All around the house you chase
To catch him is a hopeless case
But I hope he never grows up
Just stays a playful pup.

# DAYS OF INNOCENCE

From my patio I look
Down the garden to the brook
There are times when I think
I'm in a beautiful dream
As I see the children play by the stream
Young voices in joyful laughter
Chitter chatter, chitter chatter
No thought for the day after

Oh, how I remember those days
Days of innocence and carefree ways
Playing football in the park
Until it was almost dark
Those days are now gone and lost
Like an early morning frost
Days of innocence without fear
Days of yesteryear.

# A GREEN AND PLEASANT LAND

I see a world of concrete
No neighbours left to meet
Just high-rise flats
No welcome on the mats
Vast swaths of tarmac
Like some giant snake
Covers all this landscape
Oil refineries, such a blight
Blocking out the light
Pylons like giant fingers on high
Reaching out for the sky
Can no one this green and pleasant land save
Before Mister Blake turns in his grave?

# WAR ONCE MORE

Once more, again, once more
We prepare for war
Once more the young are asked
To take on a military task
But are the politicians on the front line?
Oh no, they are at home biding their time
We will fight, the politicians are insistent
But it's not them that will be blown out of existence

The politicians have a smug smile
As they look from on high
It's so easy for them for it's not them that will die
If the politicians had to fight a war
Spill their guts, shed their gore
War would be no more.

# WHISPERED SHOUT

Whisper His name
Across the valley wide
Whisper His name
Across the divide
Whisper His name

Shout His name
From high above
Shout His name
With pride and love
Shout His name

Whisper His name
From on high
Whisper His name
For you He did die
Whisper His name.

# PERILS OF A COUNTRY WALK

I walk in a field of green
All around beauty to be seen
Birds singing, such a thrill
I look behind me
Oh no! Here comes a rampaging bull!

# DREAMS

Once I was clever
But not now
I was good looking
All the girls said "Wow!"
In your sleep you see these things
Funny things are dreams!

# A DAY BY THE SEA

Little crabs hiding in a rock pool
From the young children
On holiday from school
Mums and dads in deckchairs keeping watch
Like sheepdogs guarding their flock
Barnacles linger on the rocks
Watching the children paddling
In the sea without socks.

Gulls screeching overhead
Just hoping to be fed
Children building sandcastles on the beach
Just out of the sea's reach
Sandwiches and flasks of tea
A summer's day by the sea.

# BOOKS

Books we read
Books we write
But what is this need
Of books to read
And books to write?

# FISH NO CHIPS

With broken lips and a jagged grin
Along the seabed she does swim
Her hunger drawing her in
Beneath the rocks, her prey hides
As around and around she glides
Hiding places in the wreck
She has to check

Her hunger now makes her weak
Beware for soon she must eat
Whether in the wreck or under
You cannot hide
Not from a hungry barracuda.

# A HEART BROKEN

We had a love
It was unspoken
But she was untrue
Now my heart is broken
Come the morrow, come the sorrow
Pain I don't need to borrow

My hurt is lost in time
Like my tears in the rain
Time is a healer of pain
So it's been said
But time is just a word
A word that I now dread.

# EL NIÑO

The climate is not changing, it is said
But I know different for I have seen
Desert sands covered by virgin snow
In sunlight with an eerie glow
I have seen skies that once were blue
Now darker than a raven's wing
But these birds have no song left to sing
I've seen ice caps melt with higher seas
And the higher tides that they bring
I've seen polar bears seeking humankind
For no food can they find
Starving children in drought-ridden Africa
For there I have been
Please do not tell me there's no global warming
For I have seen.

# CENOTAPH

Soldiers and politicians slowly walk the path
Wreaths in their hands to the cenotaph
With tears in their eyes they shudder a sigh
No more! No more! they cry
Will people senselessly die?
But the procession will continue year upon year
New faces, new fear
World leaders don't have the will
Can't see it's better to talk than kill
Nurses the injured will still tend
But will it ever end?
As one century ends and another starts
Can we not hope
There will be no more broken hearts?

# LOST

Lonely figure atop the moor
People searching for
Thro' driving snow he blunders on
In which direction he does not know
His name they shout but he cannot hear
To stop is his greatest fear
Freezing snow clings to his face
Slower, slower falls his pace
Valleys of snow, hills of drift
Constantly on the shift
Staggering into gullies he falls
Climb just one more tor
Lights of home shining bright
A beacon in the night
Bare trees with branches reaching out
Like sentinels to bar his way
Will he this night survive
To see yet another day?

# NO SLEEP

I have this active brain
My energy it does drain
When I go to bed to sleep
Awake it does me keep.

# NO TIME

Time gone
Time zone
Time lost
No time alone
No time to waste
All haste
Hello, sorry, can't stop
No time to talk
Must run, no time to walk
No time for this
No time for that
Must rush home to the wife
No time for life.


# PARKS (IN DEFENCE OF DOGS)

Dog
You
Poo
We all do

# LOVE AT FIRST SIGHT

The first time I saw your face
I felt lost, out of place
You took my breath away
That beautiful day
I was drawn to your light
Like a moth in the night
Your beauty so sublime
Spun my mind
Words I could not find

My heart you did capture
Enclosing it in rapture
Lost, floating in space
With the beauty of your face
The image of you
Is all I can see
Oh my love
Please be true to me.

# FIRST DAY

Along the street you walk hand in hand
You are apprehensive but also very proud
His satchel hanging down his back
Full of pencils and his dinner snack
Socks falling down his legs
'Please don't leave me, mummy!' he begs.

As you wave him goodbye
You feel such a fool
As the tears fall from your eye
It's his first day at school.

# MIRROR

Look in a mirror
What do you see?
Is the image true?
Is it really you?
When you look thro' the mirror
Do you look too far?
Is that a reflection of you
Or a distant star?
Do you have just a glance
Or do you look too far?
Can you not see
You are only what you are?

# BIRTHDAY

It's my birthday today
Another day older than yesterday
Another year gone
Where I don't know
Gone like a gust of wind
A flake of snow

Now there's grey in my hair
But should I care?
As long as it's still there!
I'm starting to feel the cold
Now I know I'm getting old.


# ON THE EDGE

Swirling clouds flying around
Red mists with no bounds
Things trying to break out
For help longing to shout
All things in turmoil
Twisting in an endless coil
Things are a must, must, must!
Is there nothing just?
Oh please, bring an end
To this my mindless trend.

# IF

If nothing is left to your senses
Your senses are left with nothing
If your eyes cannot see beauty
There will be no beauty for your eyes to see
If your heart cannot be moved to compassion
There will be no compassion left for you.


# REUNITED

Father, for you I am not sad
Though that Monday was bad
No amount of candles that we light
Your life no more can we ignite
For you I am happy
You have no more pain, anguish or fear
You have gone now no more life
You are with my mother your wife
And I know you are both still near.

# ECSTASY AND JOY

The Devil grinning just shrugs
As he feeds the young with drugs
As if they were little sweets
For them all to eat
But for their brief joy
Each girl and boy
A terrible price they will have to meet
For at the end of the day
Under a white sheet
Dead they will lay.

# I THINK TOO MUCH

As I grow old I think
As another summer flies by
No more games of hide and seek
I think too much do I
I think of the past
Of times gone by
Things I should have done
When I should have had more fun
If I had not been too shy
I think too much do I
I look at the setting sun
And think of things left undone
And I think to myself, why?
I think too much do I.

# MORNING CHORUS NO ENCORE

As the light lifts the dark
And the sun rises in the sky
Our ears perceive the song of the lark
But our eyes see the tractor trundle by
Its cargo of death on its back
Spraying poisonous chemicals all around
Killing all insects on the ground
Insects, farmers do say
Are pests to crops each and every day
But if nature was allowed its course
We would not have any remorse
For birds, their offspring would rear
With songs for all to cheer
But mothers search for food without rest
While their chicks starve in the nest
For their food that was all around
Does no more abound
The morning chorus will be no more
Morning chorus no encore.

# NO BEACH LEFT TO WALK ON

It's been so many years, such a long time
So long I don't wish to think
Many a long lonely year
Gone in just a blink
Peace beckons now at last
Just reach out and grasp

The bell has now tolled
For now I can make this journey
And be where I belong
My time now has gone
I've no beach left to walk on.


# DREAD

I have this dread
Of getting out of bed
No floor for my feet to meet
Just an empty space
Oh well, back to bed!
Leave it to others
The rat race!

# IMAGES

Flakes of snow falling thro' the leaves
Caress my cheeks, brush my tears
Chill touch of a winter's breeze
Thoughts that cannot freeze
No you anymore to tease
Gone now no more to please
The mist I now look thro'
Just leaves images of you.

# WANDERING MINSTREL

I walk the streets day and night
Playing my guitar for all in sight
Songs for all to hear
Your hearts to cheer
Many a story I have told
For all to behold
Tales of love, joy, fear
Stories to make you laugh
Cry many a tear
Emotions are what I sell
For I'm just a wandering minstrel.

# ENDLESS DREAM

Running thro' fields of endless grey
I run towards the end of day
Onwards to the end of time
Each step a step in rhyme
Clouds of grey swirling on high
Grey grass brushing my thigh
Trees of grey reaching for the sky
Thro' valleys of grey to mountains on high
Towards the distant horizon so far
Ever away from the Devil's lair
Thro' forest and thicket so deep
As grey light thro' branches creep
I see figures on horses, four in all
Running ever faster, I stumble and fall
With a deafening roar the ground opens before me
A bottomless chasm is all I can see
The four horsemen are almost upon me
I see their faces and I scream
This is my nightmare, my endless dream!

# PHOBIA

Altitude 30,000 feet
New people going to meet
Mothers with children laughing
Everyone in holiday cheer
Oh stewardess, please
Bring me a beer.

Clouds of white far below
Go speeding by
Oh, what am I doing here
So high in the sky?
Hands are shaking
My stomach quaking
I have to conquer
My fear of flying.

# NO JOKE!

My friends say my jokes are wry
They say that they are dry
But is it just a rumour
It's they that have no sense of humour?

# MOVING ON

Please don't cry for me
When I have gone
For I have not died
I have just moved on.

# HATE

Don't have ill feelings for me when I've gone
For hate is a poison that lingers on.

# HIGHWAYS TO THE SKY

Lanes meandering thro' clouds in the sky
Pathways to those who call to us from on high
Threads thro' the highways of our mind
Remind us of loved ones from another time
Ever nearer, ever nearer with arms held on high
We reach out to those highways in the sky.

# FROM A LITTLE RAIN

Dark clouds amassing on high
Rain falling from the sky
Parched earth waiting to receive
Little seeds opening an eye
Waiting to conceive
A little drop of rain
Turns that seed into corn
And corn into grain
From that little drop of rain
Our food is born.

# FOREVER GONE

The wind passing thro' the sky
Gently kissing my love goodbye
Though for me its touch does not reach
No lessons left to teach
Alone in my bed lying awake
Just counting the hours till daybreak

Day dawns at last for me to see
But what's the point – my love has left me
Love has gone forever now – at such a cost
Didn't know what I had – now all is lost
Things look different now I look back
Should have done this – done that

Life is just a series of mistakes
This I've found out – now it's too late
Now I'm left here all alone
No heart – no home
Footloose, fancy free – no ties
Though for me no long farewells
No sweet kiss *goodbye*.

# DIFFERENT

Different seasons, different seas
Different cheeks caressed by different breeze
Sun, snow, hail and rain
Falling on different terrain
Different flowers, different seeds
Different people, different needs.


# A LONG NIGHT

Candles burning bright
Long into endless night
Weary at the table he sits
New poems writing for the script.


# HELLO

I've walked this planet
For many a year
Pity no one noticed
I was here.

# TOO LONG HERE

My life was going down
Down and down, an endless drain
Until the day I took that train
Nothing to lose, everything to gain
Don't stop now, why wait?
Walk down the path, close the gate
Life here holds no more
Change that life, close that door
Just one more dice to throw
Now is the time to let go.


# WHY GOD, WHY?

I want to fly in the sky
To walk across the sea
Just to look the Creator in the eye
And ask Him, why?
Why He allows all the evil to fill the world
I look thro' my mind's eye to the past
War, murder, rape and disease
Poverty, famine and flood
This is all that can be seen
To the good people of this earth
Just trying to earn a crust of bread
Or a bowl of rice
What are their efforts worth
To have to pay this terrible price?

# HABIT

Down to the pub I wend my way
Monday, Tuesday, it's the same every day
Same faces, same talk
Don't know why I go really
Perhaps it's just the walk.


# LOVE LOST

Alone she sits by the beach
Staring out to sea
Yesterday so near yet so far away
Her love gone forever
Evermore out of reach
The boy she won, then lost
Such a terrible cost
The child that could have been ours
If we had had one more hour
But he was called to war
To see, touch, kiss her no more
For now he lies buried
On a far off shore.

# I AM

I am
I am what?
I don't know
A rose, a seed
A flake of snow
Only time will tell
If I will grow
To be what
I don't know.


# OPEN YOUR MIND

Shake off the murky waters of today
Don't be bound by the chains of decay
Today is a fever like a shroud
Blocking thoughts like a cloud
Clear the pain, clear the sorrow
Go out and grab tomorrow
Time is unforgiving of a meek heart
Grasp the nettle, make a new start.

# A HARD CHOICE

My daughter was sick day and night
Rushed to hospital in a real plight
Doctors say she is expecting a baby
No way not even maybe
She should not be ill
She takes the pill
Her life was on the line
But in time she will be fine
The baby she has now lost
Such a terrible cost
But we have to move on
The baby has now gone
The little tot is in a grave
But my daughter's life was saved
Our hearts are full of sorrow
But we have to live for tomorrow.

# A HAPPY MAN

My love for you knows no end
You're my daughter, my best friend
I'm here for you when times are bad
I'm here for you when you are sad
Here I am with advice
Because you're so beautiful and nice
Oh I am so very glad
That you chose me to be your dad.

# SAY NO TO GREEN

Celery is not supposed to be green
That colour is obscene
Celery should be white
Then its taste is a delight.

# LEAPFROG

The frog leapt and bound
But no love could be found
On and on till it was late
But he could find no mate
In the morning when he awoke
I've still no bride he did croak.

# SHORT CUT

In the dead of night
When the world is void of light
There is an eerie sound
Is it animals that abound?
What's that sound that's in reach?
Is it an owl's screech?
Not a star in the sky
Just a cold chill on high
Chilled to the bone
Need to reach home
The grounds bumpy and hard
I should have bypassed the graveyard.

# THE MESSENGER

I was in pain and sorrow
Then I met a man from tomorrow
Friend, he said, don't be down
Remove that frown
Go out, laugh and play
Make the most of today.

# NO MORE SUMMER WINE

Remember when we would walk in the dark
Hand in hand thro' the park.
Remember looking out to sea at sunset
That was when we first met.
It was love at first sight
Oh what a beautiful night!
I remember that day in my life
When you became my wife.
You gave me shelter from the storm
Your love kept me warm.
It was a wondrous dawn
The day our child was born
Now I look thro' the windowpane
Just hoping to see you again.
But no more you to dine
You are the last of my summer wine.

# THE SMILE

The touch of her lips
The colour of her eyes
The sway of her hips
Her soft little sighs
She answers the door
With a smile on her face
I know there will be more
But at her own pace.


# A BEAUTIFUL FEELING

Such a beautiful feeling
Running thro' my heart
When we're together again
After being apart
I get a tingling feeling
Just holding your hand
Running thro' my body
With the love I've found.

# THE MAN WHO NEVER WAS

Why do you all leave me alone
Living in this empty home?
I've helped you all each and every way
No matter what time of day.
You say I'm loved and adored
So why am I ignored?
I see you all pass my house by
But no one pops in – why?
When you need me I am here
But when I need love you disappear
I'm so lonely and in despair
But nobody seems to care
I feel like I don't exist
When I've gone I'll never be missed.


# CITY WHIZZKIDS

Does anyone believe
These people with their figures
And the pictures that they weave?
It's either joy and boom
With all their forecasts
Or bust and gloom

They say growth will be this or that
But these are just figures
They pull out of a hat
It's no magic wand that I wave
But if you only spend what you earn
You just might be able to save.

# NO ETIQUETTE

They fly up on high
In the hot burning sky
Flying round and round
Searching the ground
They circle hour by hour
Looking for something to devour
All shoving and nodding
Pecking and prodding
There's no grace or culture
Not with a hungry vulture.

# NO REGRETS

I suppose we had to part
Go our own way, make a new start
All things have to end
That's the modern trend
But I don't feel bad
I'm not even sad
I'll pack a bag and be on my way
For tomorrow is another day.

www.ingramcontent.com/pod-product-compliance
Lightning Source LLC
Chambersburg PA
CBHW060142050426
42448CB00010B/2258